Furry Ferrets

by Natalie Lunis

Consultant: Kim Schilling
Author of *Ferrets for Dummies*
Director of Animals for Awareness
Palos Park, Illinois

BEARPORT
PUBLISHING

New York, New York

Credits

Cover and Title Page, © Biosphoto/Klein & Hubert/Peter Arnold Inc. and Eric Isselée/Shutterstock; TOC, © Eric Isselée/iStockphoto and Orix3/iStockphoto; 4, © Cherise Gee; 5, © Diane Macdonald/Stockbyte/Photolibrary; 6, © Corbis/SuperStock; 7, © Biosphoto/Klein & Hubert/Peter Arnold Inc.; 8, (from top left) © David Brian Milne/Animals Animals Enterprises, © Wayne Lynch /All Canada Photos/Alamy, © Penny Boyd/Alamy, © Krys Bailey/Alamy, © Jevgenijs Galockins/iStockphoto, © F1 Online/Alamy, © Graham Taylor/iStockphoto, © Juniors Bildarchiv/Alamy, © Marcus Lindström/iStockphoto; 9, © Jeanne Carley/Ferret Company; 10, © Jeanne Carely/Ferret Company; 11, © Biosphoto/Klein & Hubert/Peter Arnold Inc.; 12, © Dawn King; 13T, © Stacy Lynn Baum; 13B, © Biosphoto/Klein & Hubert/Peter Arnold Inc.; 14, Courtesy of Foster & Smith, Inc./www.drsfostersmith.com; 15, © Reneé Stockdale/Stockdale Studios 16, © Juergen Bosse/iStockphoto; 17L, © Piotr Polak/PAP/Corbis; 17R, © Idamini/Alamy; 18, © AP Images/Standard-Examiner/Amanda Saslow; 19, © Juniors Bildarchiv/Photolibrary; 20, © Biosphoto/Klein & Hubert/Peter Arnold Inc.; 21, © Jeanne Carley/Ferret Company; 22T, © Eric Isselée/Shutterstock; 22B, © Jeanne Carley/Ferret Company supplied by Pacificcoastnews/Newscom; 23, © Bill Booth/iStockphoto; 24, © Orix3/iStockphoto.

Publisher: Kenn Goin
Editorial Director: Adam Siegel
Creative Director: Spencer Brinker
Design: Debrah Kaiser
Photo Researcher: Scott Rosen/Bill Smith Group

Library of Congress Cataloging-in-Publication Data

Lunis, Natalie.
  Furry ferrets / by Natalie Lunis.
    p. cm. — (Peculiar pets)
  Includes bibliographical references and index.
  ISBN-13: 978-1-59716-860-1 (library binding)
  ISBN-10: 1-59716-860-2 (library binding)
  1. Ferrets as pets—Juvenile literature. I. Title.

  SF459.F47L86 2010
  636.976'628—dc22

                    2009010378

For more information, write to Bearport Publishing Company, Inc., 101 Fifth Avenue, Suite 6R, New York, New York 10003. Printed in the United States of America.

10 9 8 7 6 5 4 3 2 1

Contents

Gotta Dance!

Pebbles opened her mouth, tossed her head back, and began to bounce all over the room. She jumped forward, backward, sideways, and sometimes straight up into the air. At one point she did a twirl, and her long body took the shape of a flying doughnut. She also made little clucking noises that sounded like *dook-dook-dook, dook-dook-dook*.

Ferrets bounce, hop, ▼ and jump around the room to show how happy they are.

4

Who is Pebbles, and why is she acting this way? Pebbles is a pet ferret. She has just woken up, and Rhonda, her owner, has let her out of her cage for playtime. Pebbles is so happy and excited that she is doing what Rhonda and other ferret owners call "the dance of joy."

Ferret owners often use the nicknames "fuzzies" and "furballs" when they talk about their pets.

Not So Wild

Are ferrets wild animals that people bring home and **tame**? Many people think so, but they're wrong! Perhaps they have the popular pets confused with black-footed ferrets—wild cousins that live in the western United States and are now **endangered**.

Only about 700 black-footed ferrets live in the wild today.

The ferrets that people keep as pets are in fact a different kind of animal. They have been **domesticated** for thousands of years. No one is sure exactly where people first started keeping ferrets, but **experts** do know why. Ferrets could do a great job of catching and killing mice, rats, and other small animals that people think of as pests. Thanks to this skill, ferrets became important helpers in homes, on farms, and even aboard ships.

▼ Pet ferrets would not be able to last for more than a few days in the wild. They need care from people in order to survive.

Many experts think that people first started keeping ferrets more than 2,000 years ago in **ancient** Greece.

7

What's That Smell?

Ferrets belong to the weasel family. Besides weasels and ferrets, this group of animals also includes minks, otters, and badgers, as well as several less familiar animals, such as polecats and sables.

The Weasel Family

weasel

mink

otter

badger

ferret

wolverine

polecat

sable

marten

All of the members of the weasel family, including ferrets, are closely related to skunks. Like skunks, they can give off a bad smell when they are frightened or overly excited. To solve this problem, many ferret owners have their pets **descented**. That means having a veterinarian perform an operation to remove the two large **scent glands** that are found under a ferret's tail. Many owners also give their furry friends a bath a few times a year to keep them smelling sweet.

Ferrets are the only members of the weasel family that have been raised by people as pets.

▲ **This baby ferret is getting dried off after her bath.**

A Ferret's Day

Ferrets play hard, but they also sleep a lot—from 15 to 20 hours per day. They don't do all their sleeping at once, though. Instead, they snooze for about four hours at a time and then wake up to eat and go to the bathroom.

Ferrets sleep much more soundly than dogs or cats. Sometimes they sleep so deeply that they seem dead!

Ferret owners need to let their furry friends out of their cages at least twice a day for up to three hours each time. That way, the **frisky** little creatures can get the exercise they need. When they're not dancing around, they pounce on loose shoes and socks, play hide-and-seek with their owners, and chase anything that rolls. They also love to explore, so they spend some of their "free" time getting into boxes, shopping bags, and dresser drawers—or any other places their curiosity leads them.

▲ Ferrets are very good at finding places to hide.

Home, Sweet Home

A pet ferret has two different homes. One is the house or apartment in which its owner lives. The other is its home-within-a-home—the cage where it stays when it isn't out exercising.

▲ A ferret cage

A ferret's little home has almost everything the furry pet needs. A cage that has been set up properly has a sleeping area with soft **bedding** and an eating area with a food dish and a water bottle. It also has a "bathroom" area with a **litter box**. Many ferret owners like to include items that will make the home more fun, such as a **hammock** for their furry friends to hang out in.

Ferrets resting in their hammock

Like cats, ferrets use litter boxes to go to the bathroom. However, ferrets are not quite as easy to **litter-train** as cats.

▲ A ferret's litter box should not be placed close to its eating and sleeping area. Like many animals, ferrets won't poop where they eat or sleep.

Ferret Food

What do ferrets eat? They eat ferret food, of course! This special kind of pet food looks like dry cat or dog food. The pieces are smaller, however. They also contain slightly different **nutrients**. Ferrets are meat-eaters like cats and dogs, but they need even more **protein** in their diets.

▼ Adult ferrets usually eat dry food. Baby ferrets—called *kits*—eat soft canned food because their teeth are not yet ready for dry, crunchy bits like these.

Of course, ferrets love to get special treats, too. Some favorites are bits of cooked meat and cooked egg. Owners have to be careful about handing out treats, though. Ferrets usually won't overeat when it comes to their regular food. When it's treat time, however, they don't know when to stop.

Ferrets like to play with their food—and their water. To prevent spilling and splashing, some owners use heavy, tip-proof bowls. Others use food bowls and water bottles that clip on to the side of a cage.

▲ **A ferret drinking from a clip-on water bottle**

Basic Training

Pebbles . . . Chuckles . . . Bandit . . . Ferret owners love to give their pets names that go with their playful personalities. Can the little furballs be trained to come when their names are called, though? Many can. The rest can learn to come running whenever they hear a squeaking sound, like the kind made by a squeaky toy.

Many ferret owners train their pets to take walks outdoors, using leashes and **harnesses**.

Owners teach their ferrets to come for a reason—to round them up when they're hiding. Other tricks that ferrets can learn are taught to them just for fun. They can sit up, roll over, and "play dead"—just like dogs. What's more, they can learn to hitch a ride on a person's shoulder—something most dogs can't do!

Ferrets can be taught to come out of their hiding places. ▶

▲ **A ferret taking a ride on his owner's shoulder**

Ferret Friends

Ferrets are friendly and playful with their owners. Often, they can make friends with other pets, too—as long as the new friend is a cat, a dog, or another ferret.

A ferret is usually more than happy to have a ferret playmate, especially if its owner gives the two furballs time to get to know each other. The same rule applies for a ferret-and-dog or a ferret-and-cat pair. The two pets need time to get used to each other.

Ferrets like to play with cats and dogs, but owners need to keep an eye on the pets in case their play turns rough.

Ferrets do not get along with pets that are smaller than they are, such as hamsters, gerbils, or birds. In fact, a ferret might be more than unfriendly around one of these little animals. It might even act like one of its wild relatives and try to kill and eat it!

Ferrets can get ▶ **along in groups, as well as pairs. Some people keep several at the same time.**

Ferret friends are usually happy to live as "roommates," sharing the same cage.

The Right Pet for You?

Lovable as they are, ferrets are not for everyone. Their playfulness often turns into **mischief**. Ferrets love to steal small objects like keys, pens, and socks and hide them. Sometimes they **nip** their owners to get their attention. They also like to squeeze into small out-of-the-way spaces and can easily get "lost" inside a house.

◀ Ferrets like to spend time in tunnel-like places, so their owners often set up all kinds of tubes and tunnels for them to play in.

Owning one of these little animals is a big **responsibility**. A ferret owner needs to have a lot of time and patience. On the other hand, there are lots of rewards for someone who is up to the challenge. This is one playful pet that will greet you with joy, make you laugh, and maybe even ask you to join it in a dance.

It is against the law to own a ferret in California and Hawaii, as well as some communities in other states. Many ferret owners believe that laws against owning ferrets exist because people wrongly think of their pets as wild animals— and they are fighting to change the laws.

Ferrets at a Glance

Babies are called *kits*; adult males are called *hobs*; adult females are called *jills*.

Fast Facts

Weight: females weigh 1–3 pounds (.5–1.4 kg); males weigh 3–5 pounds (1.4–2.3 kg)

Length: females are 12–16 inches (30–41 cm) long; males are 16–24 inches (41–61 cm) long

Colors: white, tan, silver-gray, or brown, often with different-colored markings

Life Span: 6–10 years

Personality: gentle, friendly, curious, and playful; sleeps a lot, but is very active when awake; loves to play in tubes and tunnels; likes to steal small objects and hide them

Glossary

ancient (AYN-shuhnt) very old; from long-ago times

bedding (BED-ing) soft materials used to make a place for sleeping

descented (dee-SENT-id) having an operation to remove scent glands so that an animal cannot release a smell

domesticated (duh-MESS-tuh-*kate*-id) when an animal has been bred and tamed so that it can live with and be used by people

endangered (en-DAYN-jurd) in danger of dying out

experts (EK-spurts) people who know a lot about a subject

frisky (FRISS-kee) playful and full of energy

hammock (HAM-uhk) a piece of cloth that is attached to something at each end and used as a place to lie down

harnesses (HAR-niss-iz) straps that go around the front end of animals and allow owners to hold on to the animals

litter box (LIT-ur BOKS) a box that is filled with sand or bits of paper or clay and used as a place for an animal to go to the bathroom

litter-train (LIT-ur-TRAYN) to train to use a litter box

mischief (MISS-chif) playful behavior that may cause trouble

nip (NIP) to bite lightly

nutrients (NOO-tree-uhnts) things that are found in food and needed by people or animals to stay healthy

protein (PROH-teen) a substance found in meat, cheese, eggs, and fish that an animal's body uses to build bone and muscle

responsibility (ri-*spon*-suh-BIL-uh-tee) a job; being in charge of something

scent glands (SENT GLANDZ) body parts under the tail of a ferret that can give off a strong, unpleasant smell

tame (TAYM) to take a wild animal and train it to live with people

Index

Bibliography

Bucsis, Gerry, and Barbara Somerville. *The Ferret Handbook.* Hauppauge, NY: Barron's (2001).

McKimmey, Vickie. *Ferrets (Animal Planet Pet Care Library).* Neptune City, NJ: T.F.H. Publications, Inc. (2007).

Schilling, Kim. *Ferrets for Dummies.* Hoboken, NJ: Wiley Publishing (2007).

Read More

Gelman, Amy. *My Pet Ferrets.* Minneapolis, MN: Lerner (2001).

Hamilton, Lynn. *Caring for Your Ferret.* New York: Weigl Publishers (2004).

Horton-Bussey, Claire. *101 Facts About Ferrets.* Milwaukee, WI: Gareth Stevens (2002).

McNicholas, June. *Ferrets (Keeping Unusual Pets).* Chicago: Heinemann (2003).

Learn More Online

To learn more about ferrets, visit

www.bearportpublishing.com/PeculiarPets

About the Author

Natalie Lunis has written many science and nature books for children. She lives in the Hudson River Valley, just north of New York City.